Shake and Tremor

Shake and Tremor

poems
Deborah Bacharach

GRAYSON BOOKS
West Hartford, Connecticut
www.graysonbooks.com

Shake and Tremor
copyright © 2021 by Deborah Bacharach
published by Grayson Books
West Hartford, Connecticut
ISBN: 978-1-7335568-7-3
Library of Congress Control Number: 2020950432

Book & cover design: Cindy Stewart
Cover art: © Rachel Clark, oil painting: "Lot's Wife," www.rachelclark.com
Author photo: Timothy Aguero

For John, Rose, and David

Acknowledgments

I am grateful for the deep scholarship of Dr. AJ Levine and the intellectual engagement of my fellow students in her Feminist Interpretation of Scripture seminar at Swarthmore College which informed many of these poems; the teachers who believed in me, guided me, and pushed me intellectually and artistically, particularly my mentor Stuart Friebert; all those in classes and workshops with me who offered their care and wisdom; my Poets on the Coast community; those who helped so much in the preparation of this manuscript: Kelli Russel Agodon, Daisy Fried, Susan Rich, and Heidi Seaborn; my family for all their love and support, especially my children David Palmieri and Rose Palmieri; and, for everything, John Palmieri.

In addition, thanks to the following publications which printed some of the poems that appear in this book:

The American Journal of Nursing: "The Call Comes at Midnight"

Briar Cliff Review: "Between IVF Treatments, My Best Friend Explains"

The Cape Rock: "Lot Sits at the Gates to the City"

The CCAR Journal: The Reform Jewish Quarterly: "The Day God Destroys Sodom and Gomorrah," "Drunk Under His Daughters' Hands, Lot Dreams of His Wife," "Sodom and Gomorrah the Night Before," "In the Stories Rarely Told"

concis: "Potiphar's Wife Talks About That Time"

Construction: "I Am Writing About Fucking"

Ekphrastic Review: "Morning Glory"

Floating Bridge Review: "Generations Before Lot"

Global Geneva: "Our Lot"

Heron Tree: "Lot's Wife, Now a Pillar of Salt, Addresses Her Audience"

The Inspired Poet: "As We Float Towards the Pacific, the Clouds Appear Heart-Shaped"

The Inquisitive Eater: "Salt"

Menacing Hedge: "Given a Choice," "Hagar's Banishment," "A Word for It"

Mom Egg Review: "The Polyamorous Understand You Don't Understand"

The Moth: "Today We Brag"

Offcourse: "Why I Return to Water"

Pembroke: "Women's Work"

The Pinyon Review: "The Affair"

Poetry Ireland Review: "Lot's Wife, Waiting"

The Potomac Review: "Marriage"

Sweet: "Shake and Tremor"

Typishly: "Small Lies"

Vallum: "Valentine's Day with Teenager"

Zone 3: "Farewell to His Wife"

Contents

When God Is a Woman

She does not accept apologies
for the incessant thrum.

She explains obtuse angles,
how to lay cable.

She understands that tigers eat alligators.
She set it up that way.

She rides the New York subways,
looks strangers in the eye.

She has her first child at ninety,
changes her name. It's amazing

what a woman can accomplish
when she is not afraid.

I

Women's Work

Sarai, Abram's wife, took Hagar the Egyptian, her slave-girl, and gave her to her husband Abram as a wife. —Genesis 16:3

All of them—Abram, Sarai, and Hagar—born
into a time of quiet. No
radio line hum, no buzz from broken
transformers. You could hear
the cattle in the far field.
It's hard to imagine that level of quiet,
how you could hear Abram's footfall,
how it differed from Sarai's
as it approached the flap in Hagar's tent,
the tent made of goat skin from the goat
Hagar raised and fed and chastised
and chased and eventually,
whose throat she slit.
The goat whose carcass she butchered,
meat she seared, whose hide she scraped,
softened with its own brains, her own urine
because she knew how and she could.
And now as this supple skin
Hagar stretched and tied
is lifted, it whispers *survive.*

A Word for It

The Bible gives Hagar the word that grants her
the dignity of a parasol in the desert.

What of the roots, connotations, etymology?
Words carry them around
like a Vegas hooker with her
fake leather purse of survival,
with her fake ID tucked in a plastic cover,
her real ID secured in a hidden pocket
as she high heels it through hot grit.

What the Bible calls Hagar matters.
You remember her. She is the woman
a wife gives her husband to give him the children
guaranteed by God. She's not asked
her opinion or even paid a percentage.

There's a word for it.
Not slave or servant.
Not maid.
Not concubine.

Hagar, She Who Pours Out Blood,
in service to the mistress.

Circling the Center

I stood before a stone collage. There's a word
for that. I know a word that gathers stone
into a goddess, a helix, a journey. *Slurred,*
no that's a collage of fear. *Seizure*'s a bone
collage of ocean darkness. *Cloud*'s a collage
of apples fallen in sugar. Once I stood
before those cuts in time, an open corsage
of hope and heft fitted by hands that could
fit lemons and oranges, market cries, the great
calm sweep of the sky into its rightful place.
From sweeps of molten sand, I tried to translate
the gather, the unabridged glow. Unlace
my breath *mosaic*—the word burst like champagne,
the glorious swirl of Venice, peaches, rain.

The Letter My Husband Wrote Me Twenty-Five Years Ago

He doesn't miss me much. He's scared
about his dad's heart.
He's sunk into small town
solitude.

He didn't have a date
with that other woman,
made sure it fell apart,
forgot to check the bus schedule,
that sort of thing.
He's not sure why.

He says this as if I am
an ocean away, writes
of my every body part and his,
places they will join.
He's slow, my skin smooth.

He's not sure he loves me.
He walked in the snow
and felt happy, wanted to feel
happy with me.

Morning Glory

This flower's like floating
on the moon, drifting in and out
of dreams. I am a little afraid
of all this space to be myself.

From behind the petals, I see
draw strings and scaffolds,
the magician's hat. I would have
preferred uninitiated awe.

Nuclear weapons scare me still
even though Reagan is dead, the bombs broken
into pieces we could carry in our pockets.

O'Keeffe said she would make flowers so big
New Yorkers would have to stop and see
what she sees in flowers and we all know
what she sees in flowers, the delicate opening
fold upon fold, the pink blush, the way
the shapes stretch to glory.

Today O'Keeffe would do set designs for Gaga.

I got older, slower, sadder,
came down from the clouds and found
acid rain falling. I have less hope
than I did before. I feel the dark unfold.
O'Keeffe might say we are smaller than we know,
the world more gracious.

Shake and Tremor

Still the blue heron lifts long legs over early morning.
Still the blue green boulders filled with barnacles.
Still the green ropes of sea.
Still rivulets in the sand, remnants of the night.
Still I believe in the power of lust,
the full and shake and tremor of living
on a moving planet that revolves around a ball of fire.
Still the crabs small and white like moons in need
like promises unspoken
or promises spoken and unfulfilled.
Still I wish to be swallowed whole by the sea.
Still the sea, the spume and crash of the sea.
Still the salt rich water coating my skin.
Still my porous skin.

I Am Writing About Fucking

because I am human; I am not the only one
because I like it
because sorrow was taken
because in Iran
the mullahs determine no film
with even a slight touch—
a fingertip against a cheek
a back lit shot of one shoulder
against another, a hold
even of consolation—can be made
and yet the Iranian population
tripled in the post Shah era so someone,
and why not me,
needs to write about fucking
because it is terrifying
because I am 47, but really
I would have grabbed at 27, at 17
because it's not polite and I am always very
please and thank you
because there are already
enough words for snow
because of shame, that fishbone in the throat
because we are made of stars

The Husband's Lover Speaks Up

Whose turn to romanticize
starving-artist-in-a-bohemian-attic-with-cat?
She laughs louder than they expect, then
leaves her hand on the crease of his khakis.

She chips plates, apologizes, never
black eyes them out the open window.
Sometimes she asks, *How are you feeling?*
He says *fine.*

When she reads about Hagar,
maidservant to the mother of Israel,
surrogate on command, she thinks
I'm my own sovereign.

She slips her hand
like an ace from under the deck because
do we not all strut the street
with the wind, feral?

Meanwhile she drinks lime tea
in a garden in New Jersey,
the slats of the chairs smooth against her legs.
Meanwhile a cat purrs in her lap.

Meanwhile she hefts her sighs
under the glow of Chihuly's glass ocean.
She tells herself to listen hard
for the telegraph love.

Advice from the Polyamorous

Carry toothbrushes,
condoms, a spare pair of underwear.

Love is common, tough,
but not for everyone.
Your best friend appears confused,
wants better for you, a man
to call your own. You tell her

it's possible to know your lover
takes up with another while you walk
through Chihuly's glass garden
the deep fragile edges of cobalt, feel nothing
perhaps but love.

The Polyamorous Understand You Don't Understand

I wanted a husband. The pumpkin
settles in by the dark door. She did not.
I wanted a child, sideways teeth
gone devil may care. She did not
want one of her own. We wanted
the same man but not—my son
scrapes seeds from the pumpkin
he peers in its dark depths—
on the same days. He hugs the glow
against his chest. She and I
carry this son's pumpkin,
from her condo to my porch,
her laugh skips, then jumps in
like a frog out of season.

Between IVF Treatments,
My Best Friend Explains

I want a baby. I want a baby like I want a glass of water
like a glass in my hands that doesn't shatter
not like glasses lined one after the other
with small pebbles and water
all salt.

Cast bones for me.

I want a baby more than Sarah in duty more than
Hagar who blinked. They told me to drink
herbs, iris broth. I left the dregs.
That's why my womb broke
like a glass puzzle.

Read tea leaves, Tarot.

I pee on a stick, on barley that doesn't sprout.
Who are those women who glow? I want
to steal. For this child, I will take
acupuncture like slivers of glass
in my womb.

Play the harmonium, call my child home.

I crouch by the glass in the road, broken shards. God
couldn't put this back together. I press
shards in my palm. One mandrake
root left to chew, I scramble
through old dirt to find it.

Sex in Genesis

Hagar squeezes it like a cow's teat.
The fate of the world
rests in her hands.
Abram, the father of ages to come,
shakes. As best he can,
he hauls her into his arms.
Tremors. Snot snorts out his nose.
Her ears ring.
He bites her shoulder,
she bites his, to keep
from laughing the tent down

Lies Sarai Tells About Butterflies

Their eggs arrived in diapause.
That's like taking a break from life.
Perhaps for a flood, a drought,
the inevitable scour
of Sodom. (We've heard the rumors.)

That Hagar claims no hunger for power
or money (ha!) a sour
spit I, unleavened, endure.
I found the larvae grubbing
through my stores. They crawled the walls,
fattened themselves, like a rival
can feast on despair.

I did not pin her
to a wall, demand she spin.
How could I, mere mortal,
make life begin?

Small Lies

She takes her kids to soccer, stands with them
in the rain. Church. Golden
delicious apples, dried apricots

stocked in the house of divorce she vacuums.
One night, just one night,
she lay with a stranger.

Her best friend's body an alley full of wind.
So she told her mother she offered
herself for her friend's child, a gift,

a blessing, small blue flowers on the deep
green branches, the resin so full, so rich
along the skin, the strands of hair.

Her empty friends hold her
hand through blood draws, blood pressure,
tips of the scale.

They bring the extra iron, laugh
when she farts like a lion.
They rub her feet with beeswax.

When she tears their son into the world,
branches break in her eyes.
She hurled them from her side.

Wind scrapes the bricks of her body.
It howls past gutters of blood,
rattles dark sided panes.

For the lies we tell wittingly and unwittingly.
For the lies we drape with compassion.
For lives engorged by lies.

Another Woman Sent Packing

Cast out this slave woman. —Genesis 21:10

brownish with red highlights,
no gold around the knuckles,
deep black at the creases of the knees,
no sickle cell anemia as far as can be told, but
there are no tests for Hashimoto's,
Crohn's, we just live
until we die, we chew on roots to slash the pain,
can balance water jug, pizza box, four books for
secretarial correspondence school—all on her head
while she waits in the rain for the light to change.

Hagar's Banishment

So Abraham rose early in the morning, and took bread and a skin of water, and gave it to Hagar, putting it on her shoulder, along with the child, and sent her away. And she departed, and wandered about in the wilderness of Beer-sheba. —Genesis 21:14

Before she hits the wilderness,
Hagar considers a pay phone and her last quarter
just to hear his voice.

In the growing dark,
her eyes dilate, but she doesn't need
to see to walk.

The earth curves
back in on itself, the corn stalk
grays and falls,

the pheasants poke the last seeds
until their bodies also tumble and fall
in the season of lost feathers.

Not a tree, not a small tendril
of ivy by the wisp of a stream.
Denuded earth. Abandoned sky.
Hagar still, stands.

The Affair

Tonight I walk into the desert
with one sack of water and my son.
My body an ocean I move
with the moon. I did not demand a promise.
I did not ask for my son, Ishmael

already curled in a grave-like hollow.
An angel visits me on this road to Beersheba.
Angel is the word I say when I mean
strength of will, deep and abiding conviction.
Angel is the word I say when I hear
water rise up in the well.

II

Lies Abraham Tells

I have never yearned to ride across the Japanese countryside
counting native butterflies.
I always feel blessed even on a 22-hour plane trip,
my hips trapped between the sharp edges of the arm rest,
donkeys blocking the aisles.

I did not love Hagar, did not love her strong arms, did not love
the way she turned her head when she laughed.
My wife in Pharaoh's jasmine-scented bed? I could never imagine.

I appreciate the chance to cower in a fall-out shelter.
Those shelters work against nuclear annihilation, God's anger.
I went to Canaan for the blue thread.

Seventy-five is the new fifty. I could run a Fortune 500, be president.
When the angels came to my door, I served them
cranberry scones with clotted cream.
I served the cake myself.

It feels good to do what God wants. Ask me about that day
with Isaac on the rock. When God promised me children
like the dust in the earth, like the stars in the sky, I believed Her.

Generations Before Lot, God Makes a Promise

After the flood when God's anger receded, when the ribs
of the ark broke open, when the heated dung holding
each being of the earth one to the other, crumbled
to dust, when there was an end to the endless
rocking, God touched the unicorn's bones.
She saw the fallen gnats, sweet berries
and poisonous buried in mud. She
saw the penguin's broken wing
and broke open light, benign,
beautiful her covenant:
never destroy all   again.

Lot Sits at the Gates to the City

Back pressed against the wall,
he wears a checkered jacket
even in this heat.
Who does he think he is?
He's a hustler, a go-along-
to-get-along, a war victim,
when his most honored uncle, Abram,
said, the good lands or the not
as good? He took what he wanted.
He lied for his uncle.

Tomorrow he'll be told
to leave, but he'll head back in
for the CDs, the golf trophy.
He won't know what it means,
the empty seat in the Chevy.
His daughters will see.

Not once a year, but every week
the rabbis look back in warning.

Farewell to His Wife

But Lot's wife, behind him, looked back, and she became a pillar of
salt. —Genesis 19:26

He does not look back. He does not choose
to lunge for her hand even as her hand
slips from his grasp when she looks back.

Maybe they said their good-byes
over tax returns,
a glass of wine and orange rinds.

She has done her duty: gone
to the neighbors at night,
brought back the gift of salt.

But now, as he moves forward, she
cannot. She regrets the scratches
on their records, the way

the call to glory gets shredded and flayed.
She regrets five kind words
she could have said or just her hand

slowly over his skin. She does not regret
the cost to stand. The rest of his life
he will wish for the touch of her skin.

Lot's Wife, Waiting

The war of kings
was lost. Those left
fell into tar.
She'd been captured
before.

At the camp for
displaced persons, she
waited for the Red
Cross packets of
unleavened bread,
for the child soldiers
leaning on their AK-47's,
twirling them
like white booted
majorettes
in corn country
parades, to grow bored,
fire.

She drew her name
in the stomped ground.
It's probably
still there.

Drunk Under His Daughters' Hands, Lot Dreams of His Wife

Come, let us make our father drink wine, and we will lie with him, so that we may preserve offspring through our father. —Genesis 19:32

His wife bends over the well,
the girl she was the day they met.
Warm pomegranates, her breasts.
On generous hips, her skirts
shift like afternoon shadows,
blessings of rest and sanctity.

He settles in those shadows, sips
the sweet water she offers.
Sulfur stabs—sharp, vicious. Fire rends
the tent of peace. She dissolves
in his hands.

He trembles through this dream
twice. He tastes tears.

Lot's Wife, Now a Pillar of Salt, Addresses Her Audience

The woman in the third row on the left,
the one who wishes she had
a white parasol or lived in a world
where parasols were not out of place,

you are actually paying attention.
You want to know why
I looked back. I tripped.
I caught a flash and thought

my wedding ring. I could picture
my knitting,
my frail peonies.

I had two daughters in front
and two behind.
That was my body
hanging from the city wall.

Salt

It's not bad to be compelled, held
in place like quivering ions
at the precise vertices of
a regular octahedron.
Eat this. Wear that. Pray to this God,
not the burning sun. In a face-
centered cubic lattice you know
where you are when the towers fall.

      *   *   *

You could weep
in the shadow of the well. You could
scrawl your name in neon on the night
clouds. You could walk towards or away
from a party, a prayer service.
Under sodium lights, nothing moves.

      *   *   *

Sing so hard salt whirs
off your body in pulses.

      *   *   *

The men of the cities found an unmarried girl
had helped the wandering
stranger. She gave him bread and water.
They lathered her with honey. Then they sent
bees, like salt poured from a shaker.

When We're Hard-Wired for Migration

It started with the birds,
the hole they left in the sky.

No one will make me a suit of birds,
smooth wing feathers to warm my chest.

No one will bird caress me
to the tips, soft, striated.

I have not been thinking of birds
blue-flamed. I have not been

thinking of birds in the woods even as I walk
through thin scattered blessings.

I have been thinking of the boy who likes boys
of the one night five flights up

when he pinned my arms as I begged him
to do just that. See the flame

of blue feathers. Here briefly
landed birds.

The Firmament

It was one of those summers
we climbed out windows,
swam in the lake on hot days
and days that weren't that hot.

We baked Alaska in a rented oven,
told jokes on the floor.
The jokes, the cake, exquisitely delicious.

It was one of those summers
we laughed with banjos,
sat in the front row on the grass.
Ate blueberries, sang voraciously.

We did not steal each other's lovers
or even borrow them for a few hours
in a hot dark basement.

See us there in a head to belly chain—
Mikala to Ellie to Debby
to Annie—full of matter, all aglow,
all around the world we went.

We All Have Secrets

I keep mine in an old-fashioned
treasure chest. It's pretty,
more than pretty, elegant, lined with velvet,
a domed ruby encrusted lid. At the moment,
it's sitting on the beach under a couple bored palm trees.

The latch dangles open. If you came along now,
whistling, holding a jug of rum,
it would take just a slight touch
to lift the lid, and then you'd

know that sometimes the only way
that I can fantasize myself
with another man is to imagine
my husband dead, and then
who would want me so sad?

I am looking for some chains, a good padlock.
I should bury this box. I can.

Lie with Me

And after a time his master's wife cast her eyes upon Joseph, and said,
"Lie with me." —Genesis 39:7

If you
                    won't sleep with me this time—
If you won't

Have you gotten us a room yet?
Do you want me to get it?
          Do you want to get it now?
Why don't you get it?

Won't you unzip my dress?

(unhooks her black lace bra, hands
trapped behind her back.)

I'll get undressed now. Is that all
                    right?
What are you so scared of?
Would this be easier for you
                    in the dark?

(stands with her back
to him. Lips stern, grayed out.)

I want you to come in till I get
                    the lights on.
Because I don't feel safe until
                    I get the lights on.

(The fragile bones
of her neck in stark relief.)

I will have a martini.
Do you find me undesirable?
Are you afraid of me?
That's all right. I think I
                    can understand why I'm disgusting
                    to you.
Would you like me to seduce you?

In Potiphar's Wife's Lockbox

And although she spoke to Joseph day after day, he would not
consent to lie beside her or to be with her. —Genesis 39:10

an egret feather, moon white,
the great plumed arch, prize
of hunters who stripped the wild
of its finery, once caressing
the world high
on her faithful head; a slice of sinuous
calligraphy where promises
lean in like the wind on a hot day;
the loud joyous crime of a bell in rain; the joker
from the poker game she broke up
in the servants' quarters, creased
with punch lines; her footsteps' echoes
on the empty stone patio, empty back room; the sour
of olives overbrined; her childhood
cross stitch sampler, Bless This Home
and All Who Enter; the slight sharp point
of a seam ripper.

Potiphar's Wife with Candlewax on Her Skin

1. Potiphar's Wife Considers How We Got Here

The world doesn't care if I have long hair
brushed, unbrushed, perfumed, chopped.
The world doesn't care if I samba in the park,
wear heels and eat almonds,
that my fingers are fragrant with oranges.
Why would the world care
if cholera comes across the water,
that dreams stink of dogwood?
In the beginning, Joseph was so beautiful.

2. Joseph Explains How We Got Here

I took the job because I needed the job.
That's why I've scrubbed griddles at McDonald's,
lap danced for old drunks, took the slow
Tuesday lunch shift for 2.35, no tips.
I've crawled out of pits, worn chains.
It was a full house there with Potiphar, his wife
the ten thousand candle maze.

3. Potiphar's Wife Speaks on Power

The Sphinx caresses
a riddle in his paws,
mortality. The Pharaoh hoards
rice to haul himself through
famine's realpolitik.

I have my word.

4. Potiphar's Wife Attempts to Keep a Secret

Black hairs sprout along my upper lip.
If I pluck, some man carries the word.
If you have read the story you know

what's about to happen and what will happen
after that. That's how some define God.

5. Joseph Touches My Husband

Joseph smooths the creases
from my husband's blue dress shirts,
knows the scope of his pecs,
the way doves flutter under his skin.
Joseph knots his tie in the space between
his dipping Adam's apple
and the firm ridge of clavicle
where I placed my head when we danced.
When I was young, we danced.

6. Potiphar's Wife Talks About That Time

In the end Joseph did all right for himself.
Because he was in the dungeons,
he called the dreams, and from there
he worked it like he worked it in
my husband's home, putting together
puzzles of rain, watching hands,
oh he watched, roll pastry dough
on marble table tops. I saw the oasis
shimmer at the edge of the horizon
like I had been walking toward it
my entire life, like I had been crawling
on my hands and knees.

Sodom and Gomorrah, the Night Before

A mother awake cups the moon,
takes three sips.

Her husband has been
off throwing down his luck.
Probably tried to take
the men who came through the gate,
drunk the wine
he was bound to sacrifice.

A privy door
slowly squeaks opens,
bangs shut. Shards
Still clutter the public way.

The night so dark
the lavender explodes
in whispers.

The rats don tuxedos
and waltz while Lot's daughter
sleeps with a bracelet
from her betrothed.

A muscle spasms
in the mother's chest.
She buckles, but doesn't shift
the suckling child.

Lot's Daughter Dreams the Sheep Aflame

her fingers cannot thread needle, hook, loom, she cannot
pinch out the light and feel fire smudge into her skin
shaking so hard she cannot proclaim she believes
the spark in each of us—
made in the image of the holy

cradled by Newton, one steel ball is lifted and hits, the ball
untouched flies like an angel her fingers did not lift
the first ball, every body persists in its state
except as it is compelled to change

III

The Day God Destroys Sodom and Gomorrah

God wears black leather boots, big metal hoops
at the ankles and her tight jeans with the
big metal buckle and silk in sways
of black and gray. She shaves her head.

On this day, as on all days, she commands
all notes. From her open mouth, the dark river
pours out, blood laps the shore.
She does not make mistakes.
She says, *I wish the wars were all over.*

Ten Young Men of Sodom and Gomorrah

For the sake of ten, I will not destroy it. —Genesis 18:32

There's a girl I like. I'll call her
my girlfriend. I can call her
anything I like. She'll never know.

I beat that girl because she did not know.

     *   *   *

Who read to me?
No one bought me tickets to the movies.
No one pinned my photo on the door.

My shadow cuts this land but no
water wells up.

     *   *   *

Lies float by like butterflies. I eat them.

     *   *   *

The women would not lift
their eyes to me not even when I plucked
feathers from the air.
I had, back then, nimble fingers.

The blackboard was always scratched. Rags
stuffed in the windows did not keep out the wind.
All I wanted was the peel
of an orange, just the bright tart peel.

     *   *   *

I have slept in the heat of shit piles.
I have stood outside windows.
You, with an apple in each fist, you don't know me.

     *   *   *

Monkeys with their flea filled fur
climb to freedom.
                    Not me.

Tar-digger, shadow-scraper, coin-breaker
Write me down in the Book of Raped.

          *   *   *

Boys jeered because I sucked my thumb.
I taste salt in my mouth. It comes in on the wind.
I shave. Don't say that I don't.

          *   *   *

It's not that I have greater
lungs or desert living
gives me the strength of ten.

I'd be driving my own taxi, but there are no medallions.

          *   *   *

I have visions of this land empty—no grain, no cattle, just me
stuck together with sand.
I pull open drawers, even the stuck ones, empty.

I planned for battles that never happened.
One day I looked down. I dreamt my feet had turned to pigs.

How Do You Justify Yourself?

Bash the attacker—that's justifiable
self-defense perhaps. But if you shoot
his brothers, cousins, divorced first wife,
random small children just in case, then
defense is just the excuse you give
to lick fresh blood from your fingertips.

You care about the homeland so very very much.
So you scorch lands, sow bombs, bury the axe
through your own boys' necks. You've sent the warning
to those who might storm our borders.

If someone put a gun to your head and told you
put a gun to the head of this baby (shit-spattered
or cooing your choice), would you?

If someone rocked back in his chair, tapped
one heavy black shoe and stared grim
at the unfinished list you brought in,
would you head back out, kerosene soaked
club in hand?

Milgram and Zimbardo say there's nothing
you won't do to please Daddy.

Daddy, Daddy, Daddy loves you so much
he's going to pin this medal right to your chest.
Not through the skin, ha ha,
that would be cruel.
For every hundred kills, you get a gold star.
Pizza Tuesday for the Gold Stars.
You want a statue? For that
you need to be Stalin, ha ha.

Ah yes, those fill-in-the-blanks (spit when you say it),
they are not your neighbors—the woman who brought milk,
the boy who drew spirals. They are monsters,
ogres. They have come from the bowels
of the earth. You, with a baby strapped to your back,
grab that axe, attack.

Everybody's doing it.
       Come on, baby, do the locomotion.
You probably bought a pet rock.

Can you imagine tea and toast,
a quick look in the mirror to comb your hair,
the walk to the office, straining a bit, like always,
to open the re-enforced front doors,
your comfortable chair, the line
of names neatly printed before you,
and you with your good red pen,
settling in: check, check, check.

None of which explains, Lot
offering his daughters to the mob.

What I Like About Men

What I like about men
      who Charleston is what
they do with their eyes that means did you
      want my fallacies
and loose threads, did you
      want my arms thawed, did you want
a flaming vodka to call you to
      drive ten hours and call
the sun to fall in low with myself,
      and the space of a day, my beloved?
I matched a man. Even
      as we both hit the Möbius strip. So
flung and spun. I
      curved under the night. Did
  you see me dip?
Think of the riotous color that yearns to
      open inside a tulip, feel
one soft hand on a shoulder.

Marriage

For eight hundred dollars—rent money,
a few nights at the club—the young
Puerto Rican woman with light brown hair will marry
the man from Ecuador. To the courthouse, he brings
white plastic roses and mums.

These days the standard marriage lasts five years
my neighbor said. He speaks from experience.

What I'm trying to say is despite the heart and lungs
and the same rotating shoulders
in their ball and socket joints, we cannot
understand each other.

I cannot understand why an Indonesian man
would leave his betrothed to study
accounting in Austin,
why a banker would end her marriage
to adopt a child.

After the CEO's ex-wife died, he
telecommuted and cooked
for the children he left three years before.
There was, it seems,
a reconciliation during chemo.

Strokes, biopsies—some weeks all my students
have family emergencies.
It was just a little bit of cancer Nicole tells me and pinches
her thumb and finger together. I match her casual distance.
My mother too I say, and we go on
to Chris' father who drinks too much.
But this week, everyone is getting married!
Amal proclaims marriage
the basic unit of all happiness.
Matt glows. Svetlana blushes.

I am waiting for the five-year update
when the friend says to *The New York Times*,
After that break up I never thought
they'd get back together.

At the wedding reception, there were daisies
with purple ribbons. There were cupcakes.
We tangoed and two-stepped. We waltzed.

Today We Brag

Truth, beauty, what else
did I sneak into my pockets?
Oranges. Honey.
I overflow.

If you'd heard the cardinal
sing, you too would have
built your hair into a chiffon.
So gray, so what, my hair.

For every minute you waited,
I did not wait. Lay it down blessed,
Hafiz, lay it down, and I thank you.
You didn't have to love me
like you did but you did
and I thank you. I will attest
to the stubborn rain.
I could be beaten dead
by the Battle Royale.

All of this is more than we
can understand, we
who are hungry, come
further than we can
fathom, I declare all can,
should, will.

The Call Comes at Midnight

You get the news in the corridor.

Your eyes slide down
the sterile washed-out
green walls outside

the room where your father still breathes. The door
not even closed, just a curtain of birds
with sharp beaks between you.

You get the sharp news
in the airport bathroom, the faucet broken,
the hand towels stuck, a small boy
almost overbalanced
by a blue Elmo suitcase as he walks
alone toward the door.

You get the new news, and the flights are all booked.

You remember that boyfriend of your mother's
who didn't die of being drunk.
You remember the day you drove
angry in the rain, the pool of oil on the road.
You remember black stitches, blood
seeping at the edges.

You get the old news, and you must
wrap dishes so they don't crack.
You write out your full name. When you get
the devastating news, a large liquid silence
tries in vain to devour the skin of the sky.

Valentine's Day with Teenager

A teen died last week.
Not my son. This is
not a scene I can describe.

He left a note. I have not read it.
Gun, knife,
pills, I don't know.

We have no guns. We have
knives, a roof. *Are you
suicidal?* I ask my son.

Chocolate hearts cool
on the rack. He baked them for
his friends.

A teen died. Not my son. *Are you ever
suicidal?* He gave me a heart
as he left the house
this morning.

My Thoughts Before Death

I should have swum in the culvert,
picked daisies and dandelions from
cement cracks.

I wish I'd fished the dream river, held on
to math and Latin.
I should have bowled more and better.

I wrote you a letter the day
I found out you had AIDS. This is back in the day
T cells fell like North Dakota mercury,
but not as pretty.
I didn't send and then
pale skin, skin like raw silk, oh bones
with only sunlight for skin.

Make sure I have a hat, wool socks
maybe those little hand warmers.
When I am without words, know
I am always cold.

I Asked My Friends What Happened When They Tried to Pack Up Mom

We packed up Mom but I couldn't part
with *The Speakable and Unspeakable
in Quantum Mechanics*, the word of God,
The 1922 *History of the Modern World*.
I needed to know 1922.

From my mother it was all the diaries and letters
of Woolf, Whitman's gilt edges, the stained binding—
Lesbian Nuns: Breaking Silence.

3 boxes of shower curtain rings
an untouched lifetime supply of BRECK
place settings for 118
27 pairs of black pants
all her notes from college music, mimeographed
I smell the effort, the desire
100 used incandescent light bulbs
a bathtub full of pinecones

in the last drawer we looked in, handmade
string puppets, the nativity scene
papier-mâché, peeling paint, half-smiles,
the cow and lamb who lost their tails long ago.

They met on a round-the-world cruise. It read
like an ad "met young Mr. Hatfield on deck,
toured Cheops, shopped for rings in Africa."

I found my father wrote my mother
romantic letters years after they
divorced, married others.

Opening an album, we found
a card from dad
and the flower she dried and pressed
from their first date, the first poem
he wrote her. The house
grew silent, the air heavy.

We held the corsage
from their wedding.

Mom asks me to read
my journal to the world,
the speakable and unspeakable.
I plan a soirée, perhaps a séance.

Our Lot

Can you feel the lid screw into the threads?
Cloisonné turns once, twice, locked.
You aren't dead yet. The thing with the hip
just a displacement, not the end.
There will be an end; this coalescence
of atoms will dissipate like a song
from David's harp, a car chase
through Grendel's cave where
the faces barely shake.

Lot tied a string to the table leg.
It unwound past where he refused
to stay. Out of the caves,
it wandered the lineage with him.

We eat the tangled grasses of the dead.
We wear the flowers of the dead.
We smoke long pipes with the dead.
We make claims for the dead,
follow the thread.

In the Stories Rarely Told

The ox awakens, ears ring
from the bellows in his dreams.
He lowers his broken
horns and walks.

The ox comes slowly, swishing
his long pink tongue.
Dust and flies ride
his hooves as he plods.

He does not dread. He does
what he must: lick.

From her crown to her tendons,
to the hard ridges
of her toes, Lot's wife
all ferocious salt. Hard grains
send up small rockets
as she dissolves.

As We Float Towards the Pacific, the Clouds Appear Heart-Shaped

Now that we've moved to Seattle,
we will buy copper river salmon steaks
on sale at Safeway for $4.95 a pound,
pink and thick, eat them
Wednesdays when the sun shines.

We will scrub the spider webs of North Dakota
from our bumpers, the dead bugs of Montana
off our grill.

You fold the cardboard I carry
to the curb. I cut grass.
You bake bread.
We fix the broken freezer.

You are my paper marigolds, my Marco, my Polo,
my new blue swings.
You are river stones in the garden.

If this were the last day, still
where I would choose to be,
the ocean near our backs.

How will I remember you
in twenty years? With grapes in hand
you say, grapes in hand.

Why I Return to Water

Long twists of bull kelp.
I fill them like a *shofar*,
tekiah silver sharp,
shevarim, the curve of the shore,
teruah, the curve of the sky.

I bury my body in sand.
Dribble a bit on my leg and pause.
I try again, dig deeper and now
my legs start to merge
with day and night, with what shifts
and settles.

Deep in the ocean, sand,
remnants of kings and decrees,
the code of Hammurabi,
comes to write on my skin.

The oceans just barely alive.
The moon pulls
waves through my body.
Something will come to me
a seagull, a grain of sand.

I will know my place in the world.

Notes on the Poems

I used the New Revised Standard Version for all Bible quotes.

A Word for It: I am indebted to Philip R. Drey and his article "The Role of Hagar in Genesis 16" for the research that informed this poem.

The Day God Destroys Sodom and Gomorrah: The last line is from a traditional folk song of the same name. I am inspired by the Tim Eriksen version.

Lie with Me: All lines not in parentheses are from Mrs. Robinson in *The Graduate.*

Why I Return to Water: A *shofar* is a ram's horn blown as part of the Jewish high holy days. *Tekiah, shevarim,* and *teruah* are names for three of the blasts.

Additional Information on Biblical Stories

God promises **Abram (Abraham) and Sarai (Sarah)** they will have many descendants. However, Sarai does not conceive, so she demands Abram take her enslaved servant Hagar in her stead. When Hagar becomes pregnant, Sarai is unkind to her, and Hagar runs away. An angel speaks to Hagar, urging her to return and promising her many children. Hagar returns and gives birth to Ishmael. Meanwhile, God renews the promise to Abram and Sarai and changes their names to Abraham and Sarah. Sarah at ninety gives birth to Isaac and soon after insists Abraham send Hagar and Ishmael away.

In the story of **Sodom and Gomorrah**, God promises not to destroy the cities if there are ten good men in them. There are not. But the angels who will rain fire and brimstone on Sodom and Gomorrah go to Lot (Abraham's nephew) and promise to spare him and his family if they leave and do not look back. Lot's wife looks back, and God turns her into a pillar of salt.

Later in Genesis, Joseph is sold into slavery in Egypt and becomes an overseer for **Potiphar**, one of Pharaoh's officers. Potiphar's wife tries to seduce Joseph, but he refuses. She then falsely accuses him of rape.

Lot's wife and Potiphar's wife are unnamed in the Bible.

About the Author

Deborah Bacharach is the author of *After I Stop Lying* (Cherry Grove Collections, 2015). She received a 2020 Pushcart honorable mention and has been published in journals such as *Poetry Ireland Review*, *Sweet*, *The Carolina Quarterly*, and *The Southampton Review* among many others. She is an editor, teacher and tutor in Seattle. Find out more about her at DeborahBacharach.com.

CPSIA information can be obtained
at www.ICGtesting.com
Printed in the USA
LVHW051135160321
681669LV00021B/851